THE SOJOURNER

SELECTED HAIKU

BY

STEFANIE BENNETT

ISBN: 978-93-90601-86-8

First Edition: 2022
Rs. 200/-

Cyberwit.net
HIG 45 Kaushambi Kunj, Kalindipuram
Allahabad - 211011 (U.P.) India
http://www.cyberwit.net
Tel: +(91) 9415091004
E-mail: info@cyberwit.net

Printed at VCORE CONNECT.

Learn about pines from the pine

And about bamboo

From the bamboo.

BASHO

ACKNOWLEDGEMENTS

Some of the poems have been published in the following:

UFO Gigolo – Open Mouse Poetry – Westerly Magazine – First Refuge – The Foundation of Australian Literary Studies – Poems of Social Justice – Madness Muse Magazine – Alice Springs News – Beyond the Rainbow Literary Magazine – The Four Seasons (Anthology) – Every Writer's Resource – Reflections – Southerly Magazine – Shattered (Anthology) – Dissident Voice [A Radical Publication in the Struggle for Peace and Social Justice] – Haggard and Halloo – Chicago Reader – Literary Responses to Asia – Dead Snakes – The Angelo European - Ink – Sweat and Tears – Kind of a Hurricane Press – The Galway Review – In Between Hangovers – Degenerative Literature – Plum Tree Tavern – Eskimo Pie – Illuminations Galerie France - I am Not a Silent Poet – Project Agent Orange – Verse Writes – Poetry Pacific – The Maleny And District Collective – Every Day Poems – Mad Swirl – The Best of Mad Swirl 2018 (Anthology) – Your One Phone Call – Orbit Net – Echonetdaily – Grey Sparrow Press – Ecord – Our Day's Encounter – The Australian – Lady Liberty Lit – Poetry Super-Highway – Pangolin Review – Poet Of The Week – Harbinger Asylum Magazine – Annual Holocaust – Remembrance Day 2018 Collection – Scars Publication – Lochraven Review – Rasputin – A Poetry Thread – Transcendent Zero Press – Ilya's Honey Quarterly – Haiku – Haiku Universe – Electronic Pamphleteer – Poetry 24, and others.

ABOUT THE AUTHOR

Stefanie Bennett has published 25 volumes of poetry. Over 50 years, she has acted as a publishing editor, tutored in The Institute of Modern languages (James Cook University) … and worked with [No Nukes] Arts Action for Peace.

Of mixed heritage (Irish/Italian/Paugussett-Shawnee), Stefanie was born in Townsville, North Queensland Australia in 1945.

Stefanie, an ex-blues singer and musician, has been fluent internationally in poetry online and in print journals. She has been nominated for the Best of the Net and The Pushcart.

Once again, a very large thankyou to those who have supported my work of words over the last few years. I thank you for the time you have given me. Also, in 2007, the coming together of Australian Groups ie; ACF,CFA, Arts Action for Peace and others, joined the call for a 'nuclear free world'.

ICAN – The International Campaign to Abolish Nuclear Weapons was born.

I am proud of and indebted to my lot for having won the 2017 Noble Peace Prize.

TIME LINE QUOTES

'Ms Bennett is perhaps one of least recognized important poets of the new wave.'

(Thomas Shapcott – The Australian)

'Thank goodness somebody thinks poems are forever. You go back to Dickinson'

(Judith Wright – Black feather)

'Stefanie Bennett writes poetry with a capital P. Not for her the rueful ironies and domestic incidents that make up so much of her contemporaries' work. She insists on a bardic voice, an unapologetic moral purpose and a communion with artists and true poets wherever and whenever they may be found.'

(Penelope Nelson – Quadrant)

'With everything about her the maverick, her most recent book – *The Hermit in Translation* –executes a deep bow to tradition. Here Bennett's own voice is found at liberty, possibly too, a note of Dorothy Auchterlonie's principled humanity. This is a daring leap, and innovative.'

(Judith Rodriguez - Poetry Editor Penguin Books)

"Beyond Bennett's undoubted technical skills however, is the quality, which elevates her to the top rank of Australian poets. It is the way she effortlessly (well, apparently effortlessly, - *ars celare artis*) enmeshes language and land, showing both to have value beyond their capacity for exploitation, showing both are inextricable aspects of humanity and human survival. In this, *Symphony for Heart and Stone,* ranks with Chris Mansell's *Mortifications and Lies,* Peter Minter's *Blue Grass* and John Kinsella's *The New Arcadia,* as a fine example of a kind of 21st century poetry that is not only relevant, but essential in a world, and especially a nation where language, land and humanity are consistently being abused"

(Tim Thorne)

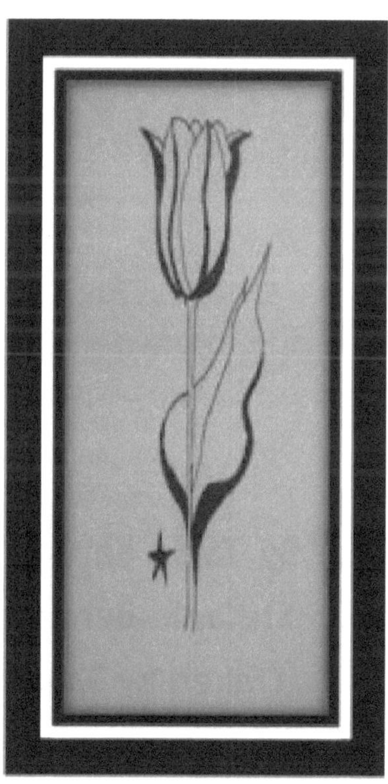

Cover Photo: By Tania Kavney

Rear Photo: Stefanie Bennett

(Taken by Tania Kavney)

APPEASEMENT

There in the halfway house
in the rain -
the Rosetta Stone

SPECIAL MENTION

On my laptop screen
a frog
in waiting

LUCIDITY

Thinking of home a wanderer
joins the cuckoo's
cry

THE NUMBERS

Tree
hugging
tree

WAR WAGON COM.

The fare-thee-well silence
speaks
relentlessly

SOCIAL JUSTICE

What would the world be
if it hadn't
betrayed the rose

THE BRIEF

Entombment reading –
the tealeaves in
Latin

TONIGHT

Singing in the rain –
a creaking
mailbox

FERTILE EARTH

The visible haiku
takes off
her shoes

PILGRIMAGE

It's neither here
nor there;
the never never

REALIZATION

I don't want a New Year –
I prefer
the old one

TELESCOPE

Moving into The Hood
the huntsmen
spider

MORTALITY

Old fashioned music –
typewriter
keys

LIGHTNING FLASH

A Winter rain's
heavy
heart

PREVIEW

The remains of the day –
writing myself
a letter

THE FORCE

Sun-up… white wisteria
in the raven's
beak

RENT A TEXT

End of the year still
stuck with
the first of the last

HUMAN AFFAIRS

How to fix
a three legged
bed

LEGACY

Sand in the car boot –
a time
to remember

CONQUEST

Old heart, young love
the depth
of it

SPRING'S VENUE

On opening the door
the skyline
enters

MODE OF LIVING

It's a given; just
return me to
the book store!

QUIRKS

A tertiary
rainbow
on the run

GALIXY LOSS

The intoxicated
mobile
phone

FRAILTY

Land and sky
sleep
side by side

COLD CASE

One naked gun
looking for
its holster

SPIN DOCTOR

Telling a fish
how to
swim

HIGHER POWER

A sun swept Lake Pedder
lies pocketed
in the backwoods

VERSE FORM

The caw of the crow -
syllables
of daylight

JOURNEY

Death's distant sunset -
the riderless
horse

'BONJOUR'

Thinking about you
one thought
deserves another

CONTATA

A pale throated sloth
hums Puccine
off key

STORM BREWING

Taken to flight -
the feather
bed

ANCIENT SHARDS

Breathe in deep -
where
does the time go

THE ANGEL

No text; who am I
WRITING
FOR!

HOUSE HUNTING

Wear dark glasses
and wield
a big stick

ENTWINED

Tears of the sun -
the sound
of the flute

SORROW

In the vacant seat
the last word
uttered

POSTAL DELIVERY

A buzzing
mud
wasp

SOUND SYMBOL

Running on empty -
the stuck
elevator

INTRODUCTION

The shooting star
scatters
the evening news

THE FIREFLY

AH! This forthcoming
old age
passes quickly

ATTENTION

Stepping out of line
the grass tree
spears

SPECTRUM

The kindness cloud
above
an infinite sky

DAWN

Me and my shadow
limp
lightly

REQUEM

Universal desire;
modest
Winter Wood

HOPSCOTCH

Twitter followers
in witches'
hats

THE CLASSICS

Haiku and Zen –
my brother's
keeper

AFGHANISTAN

Just another
bullet proof
vest

BELL RINGER

Identity politics
calling all
ghosts

INSCRIPTION

Summer rain
puddles
hallucinate

HUMBLE FARE

Stepping stones –
the way
of the lotus

CO-CREATOR

When saying farewell
the mind is
a camera

SENSORIUM

Strange knocking -
the leaves
at my door

FAUX PAS

A fascist in
our rank
of pranks

SEPTEMBER MOON

The drunken lifeboat
one voice
singing

ALL FALL DOWN

My wisdom tooth's
not
working

PEACE ACTIVISTS

Wild flowers
on the road
again

IDEOGRAM

Some are born with fists
instead of
fingers

WIKIPEDIA

Another whispering
snail
gate

HEADLINES

An energy market
chasing
a 'sun tax' ?

LIGHTS OUT

Creaking window –
my deceased
sister

MODE OF LIVING

Designer love –
an empty
hammock

LOTUS LEAF

Cold Mountain poems
like clover
over and over

CAPTAIN'S CALL

No smart phone
out smarts
a doting eagle

SIGNPOST

Destiny's child –
the void of
all that is …

EVOCATION

That red moon arrives
along with
the devil

BALANCE

Daylight's daughter –
the fallen
flower

ILLUSION

Nothing is never over
just repeat
a line of sleet

STEP BACK

Over night collision –
space junk
on the rebound

DELIBERATION

Fox and hound
happy to be
together

THE FOIBLE

Time after time
a monkey mask
gets torn

THE JOURNEY

A motorhome towing
both hammer
and sickle

CONUNDRUM

Time can't stand still
on one
leg

THE PHOTOGRAPH

Say Cheddar
or
Brie

CORPORATE WORLD

Snail Gate
slip sliding
away

OBSERVATION

Becoming the hourglass –
the Navajo
moon

TOM THUMB BLUES

It's just a shadow
we hide
behind

LIGHTNING CLASH

Swallows in the eaves
deliver
gorilla grams

10,000 THINGS

A cloud covered
Zazen's
thatched hut

DUETS

In the eye of the frog
the pending
half moon

PROCISION

A mosquito buzzing
the blues
away

PAPER CHASE

The recent past
now the most
distant future

ALIEN INC

Freedom of form
in a cat's
whisker

SILHOUETTE

The raven within
remembers
Nagasaki

ROM tester

Beamed up … a set
of moral
principles

BLING

Hands need a handle
to hold
water

FOG BOUND

Getting over myself –
violets
into dust

SUMMIT

A chorus of blackbirds;
the eye
of the sky

CARBON COPY

Seen on the lip of time
the embattled
rose bud

POST MODERNISM

My conversation with
a chrysalis
I will not tell

BELLINGEN ISLAND

The flying fox flits past
Gaea's
moon face

FOOTPRINTS

A crimson rosella
bringing
the inside out

TEMPLE

Atop the ant hill
the purple
iris

WORRY BEADS

The bucket list
went
walk about

CASH AND CARRY

It's what didn't get said
that matters
most

GREGORIAN CALENDER

Cry freedom … there's
one flaming star
down

OLD WARRIOR ASKS –

Tree stump
how do
you do?

SURROUND SOUND

Claw deep in cloud
the red winged
hawk

EQUATIONS

Afternoon tea –
the tarmac's
no fly by

OCEANIA

Nothing to disclose
but the stone jaw
of Rapanui

SWAT TEAM

Falling asleep
the day's
reckoning

FALCON DREAMING

... World on fire –
a Harvest Moon
endorsed it

MIST PASSING

Dream writ –
rainbow
logic

ENVIROMENT

Sweet nothing –
the arm's
race

THE PASSING ERA

Unable to step back
night time planets
begin to speak

SPIN OFF

Scarecrow entwined in
windswept
moon glow

NASA (DOWN UNDER)

Hitting a nail
on
the head

COLD WAR 2

The lone geranium
in the field
of fury

THE GREY

Tethered to the barber pole
a long haired
retriever

TRILOGY

An ivory carnation
black belts
the lawn mower

INSIGHT

Unattended note book
correcting
the rhyme and spine

OTHERNESS

Raindrops on the roof –
spirit
drumming

HOWZAT (how's that)

A lizard playing
'dodgem'
on the pitch

MOONRAKING

Fair crack
of
the whip

THIS TIME

Goodbye again; the dusk
has no reason
to grieve

GLOBALISATION

Civil Rights
worldly
wounded

OAHSPE

The 'Tree Of Life'
becomes
a sitcom

STUCK

A spanner in the works
doesn't
work

UNFORGETTABLE

The talking book
that won't
shut up

AFGHAN 2; GROUNDSWELL

Can't find the thin
edged wedge
know how

CULTURE THE WAY IT IS

Hitching a ride on
the wheel barrow
a garter snake

LAW AND DISORDER

The dish did indeed
run away
with the spoon

COUNTRY

This year's a stand still –
I stir the coffee
with my thumb

SENRYU

The mother of all
mosquitoes
slaps back

LIGHTNING RIDGE

Water lilies
walking
on water

MACHINERY OF POWER

The Beetaloo Basin
alludes to
green ant dreaming

WEAR AND TEAR

Is it spring or sprung –
this existential
wind chime

MASQUERADE

Walking… talking…
the eclipse
of the heart

CONSTELLATION

The breeze got caught
in the middle
of a quarrel

INDECENCY

Box cars –
flashing
lights

ICON

Karaoke koala
the way
she talks

HOLLYHOCK NATION

Just a Café Mocha
energized
by a sunbeam

HIROSHIMA

Winds in the pine
past and
present

SIMPLICITY

New days come
out from
under

BORDER SECURITY

Climb
every
mountain

FOUNTAINHEAD

The umbrella
searches
in the rain

STAYING ALIVE

Living is an
occupational
hazard

BREAKING EVEN

A blunt
point
of view

CROW'S CALL

Memory
has it
a silhouette
for two

AMONG THE ROSES

All the colours
between
black and white

THE ORBITER

Walking away I leave
myself
behind

EBB TIDE

In need indeed -
hand that moon
a torch

FUGITIVE

Cloud faced -
a daisy
felled

THE GOOD LIFE

Peach tree blossoms
and the cuckoo
passing

SPRING

Rain talk got me
thinking
laterally

CONVALESCING

The cat's grin
obstructing
the moon

EACH SEASON

Speaking your name
I rearrange
the photo frame

BREXIT

... The war
of
The Shrubs!

COSMIC SHOWER

It's just Chief Joseph
taking care
of business

AURORA BOREALIS

Long time gone
house
of song …

THE CLASSICS 2

Gentile centipede
romancing
the stone

FOOL PROOF

The half moon and I
share
the same rocker

ITALO

Baking beans;
nothing left
to hunt

EPIGRAM

Yeti's paw print-
the orb
of the sun

ONE-NESS

The sound of goodbye
laid to waste
the ebb tide

NOON TIME

Two differing colours-
the farm dog's
eyes

THE LULL

Eventide calls-
a dandelion
does push-ups

ANCESTORS

No victory
without
loss

CLIMATE EMERGENCY

Once we were young…
too old for
the killing fields

RE-READING 1984

Dante's
cart wheeling….
derby

THE PACIFIST

Call 'the sandman'
a raindrop's
crashed

INDIGO YEARS

A snapdragon's
tough
weed hood…

FIXATION

Mail stamped
'return
to sender'

REBELLION

The hazy sun fell off
God's cat daddy
wagon

TROUGH

Let's call a truce -
the old woman
and the sea

PRETENDING TO BE ME

A blithe spirit;
the bearded
stranger

HUMAN AFFAIRS

Sin city…
apple
turn over

COMMUNE

The grass spear; it's
a wayward ant's
freeway

EVOLUTION

So lonely talking
into
the cat's ear

STONEHENGE

What's to come carries
itself
away

DIVINE VISION

As the kettle whistles
the butter knife
curtsies

USSR; AKHMATOVA'S 1966 RETURN

'All those who tampered
long before
apply within'

DEMOGRAPHICS

Look! The two pine trees
grow nearer
together

REVELATION

Foretold; the hairbrush
is having
a grey day

FATE

Waiting on the phone
to pick me
up

PRECISION

It split the axe handle -
a cracker
of a frost

THE POCKET DESKTOP

The book of Change
or failed
revisioning?

SUBTITLES

Run away rogue…
attention in
detention

REALM

Lilacs in the sand -
still life
hallucinates

PROJECT

Dog days…
a postman
on the run

THE COLOUR OF DAWN

Where's the ocean-
life's too short
for comfort

CALLING ALL ANGELS

The
Body
Bag

CROWING

Watch your head
it's what
the sky said

SCORE

Warring for peace;
like the slug
I'll nap on it…

TIME TRAVELLER

Never having
to say
sorry

BEDAZZLED

Reflective store front
mirror;
don't look back

TRANSLATION

Reading a teacup -
the headlines
carry guns

EARTH WATCH

Midlife-
cobwebs
and clover

SYLLABLE COUNT

Tombstone?
who goes
there…

DAY BY DAY

The razor
wire
song

ELSEWHERE

Hanging from the disc
of the moon -
a heart is breaking

THE FLUX OF THINGS

At my journey's end
only the heron's
cry amends

TREASURE

Storm shelter
the buck-some
willow

WINGS

Whoever we think
we are
we are not

CREATION

Out of the Autumn wind…
earth mothering
violets

HILLOCK

The monkey mask
frightens
the monkey

ORCHID BREATHING

This new year's hermitage
goes beyond
the pale

EVENT

Stacking the pantry
my old glasses
found me

STATE OF THE NATION

The political play book
of
bubble and squeak

SPACE TIME

Black holes
in
the sunset

NUTS AND BOLTS

A scam is a scrum
in any
definition

FOCUS

The forgotten
tail of
the frog

EITHER WAY

Leap Year fell
over
itself

ATTENTION

Fox in the headlight -
is that you
Kerouac…

NONETHELESS

The inside out dream
lets sleepless
dogs be

ASSERTION

The crooked pine
has got
my spine

LATE EDITION

In the cupboard the worn
sweat shirt
of mourning…

CLASSICISM

The coming attraction
a mosquito
hums
Mozart

QUEST

A hitch-hiking haiku
texts
Issa

THE FOX

Nonchalant facing
of winter's
passing

HAZE

The art of forgetting
not written
yet

COMPLETENESS

Cushioning the half moon
the most
distant of lovers

REFLECTION

No doubt about it
the sour dough
is on the rise

SKILL

A hard hat quietly
looking for
its head

BOUNTY

The magenta Buddha
handshakes
the morning glory

TIDE

At world's end? The words
I would
leave you

OBSERVATION

An aged mulberry tree
attracts
snakes & ladders

CULTURE

What a cracked lid -
the coffee
grinder

FRACKING

The drill bit
tortured
my teeth

TEA FOR TWO

A cash splash
who needs
it

THE BACK COUNTRY

Sunrise seen through
a bandicoot's
ears

REVIVAL

High noon; the summit
in my back
pocket

VISUALLY ACTIVE

The drone's got
a no parking
ticket

OBSERVATORY

A carnival of fireflies
in a lamp lit
stairwell

HUMAN AFFAIRS

Give and take -
ebb
tide

VOYAGING

Between 'Mice And Men'
Steinbeck's
temple gate

HEAT WAVE

Not much to do;
go hose
the salamander

WIPEOUT

Strong winds; the house
gets up
and walks away

NIRVANA

The empty mail box
talks to
the animals

MORNING GLORY

Head in the sand
I am
what I am

THE REAL WORLD

Family at a loss -
I kept
the Bodhi tree

NIGHT'S TOWN CRIER

Evolution yawns in
a purple
dawn…

MIND SPORT

Philosophy

in

rags

IN 'EDO

The fly writes Taoism
with
her feet

WOKE!

Nah… go back
to where
you belong

SALVAGE

Home alone
we begin
to speak

UKRAINE

The heart of the matter
a dog star's
referendum

IN MOURNING

Hell fire kicks
the bucket's
runaway moon

WEALTH

Coins in my pocket
don't mean
a twist of fate

AUSPICIOUS DAY

Cricket voices
landing
on Mars

SUN SET

The tea ceremony
following
a thunder clap

RAPTURE

Platypus -
water
music

NO HUMBUG

Daughter to Zeus -
she climbs
mountain

DIVINE COMEDY

Press gallery
all of one
mind

SOLITUDE

Dust never settles when
the loved one
passes

FLAGSTONE

The ghost of old
sorrow -
river's end

LIGHTNING HAZE

Two strikes
are better
than none

BIBLICAL BEINGS

Bats flying
to hell
and back

SKY NEWS

Under cloud cover
the ghost fed
clover

INCANTATION

Stuck in the empty
wine vat
the dead poet

TEDIUM

Another life away
liberty's
dying

JUXTAPOSITION

The tree stump chained
to a dog's
collar

REVELATION

Shape shifting again -
the cracked
mirror

HUSH

Another sliding door
doing
a runner

BOAT WOMAN

A lot on her mind -
the crone
flies backwards

QUILL CALL

Wind swept
tiger
lilies

A SKY BURIAL

Wisdom is the cart
before
the horse

BEWITCHED

The drainpipe hit
the ground
running

DOWNLOAD

Arms-race! Nothing
to do with
heart and head

METEOR PROGNOSIS

Montezuma's at
tomorrow's
hard rock cafe

NUCLEAR SCIENCE

An uncivil war…
riches
and lust

REFERENCE

It's a conundrum; not that
I miss you
but by how much

MULTITASKING

The aged orbit the earth
before
leaving

MOON WALK

Circuit breaker -
I believe in
nine lives

INSIGHT

Mix with fools
you will
learn

THE LUCKY COUNTRY

A spillover of rain
again
from the poor box

THE UNDERSTUDY

Grandma's mashed potato
taught me
how to dance

FULL MOON

Hush, the string bean
is
listening

EULOGY

In the province
of the heart
Buddha's shack

OVERHEARD

And all you ever got
was what
you wanted?

BACK WATER BLUES

Skipping stones
love me
love me not

DIAGRAM

Remembering your face
in asset rich
firelight

HEAVEN'S GATE

World speak… what
does she say?
Run…

LANTERN PARADE

Strange bedfellows
the harp &
the king

ACTIVITY

Among the daffodils
the barking mad
kelpie

HOPSCOTCH

The aged pay phone
knows only
rainy day people

STAR WALKER

Sobriety's
straw
woman

COMMONPLACE

Chasing satori
I stub
my toe

BRAIN DRAIN

The apostrophe
has become
rocket science

KARMA PROBLEM

Blackened toast
white
tablecloth

ENIGMA

A fiddle weeps -
strings
too tight

GOOD GRIEF

A caterpillar
mid field
growing old

SHADOW LAND

Visibility; the heartbeat
breaks
the fall

BECOMING DUSK

Empty elevators
leave
the building

* 9 7 8 9 3 9 0 6 0 1 8 6 8 *